Healing from Infidelity: *A Guided Journal*

HEALING FROM INFIDELITY

A Guided Journal

Prompts and Practices to Help You
Recover and Move Forward

Tamara Thompson, LMFT

ROCKRIDGE PRESS

Copyright © 2022 by Rockridge Press

All rights reserved. No part of this publication may be reproduced, stored in a retrieval system, or transmitted in any form or by any means, electronic, mechanical, photocopying, recording, scanning, or otherwise without the prior written permission of the Publisher. Requests to the Publisher for permission should be addressed to the Permissions Department, Rockridge Press, 1955 Broadway, Suite 400, Oakland, CA 94612.

First Rockridge Press trade paperback edition 2022

Rockridge Press and the Rockridge Press logo are trademarks or registered trademarks of Callisto Media Inc. and/or its affiliates in the United States and other countries and may not be used without written permission.

For general information on our other products and services, please contact our Customer Care Department within the United States at (866) 744-2665, or outside the United States at (510) 253-0500.

Paperback ISBN: 978-1-68539-296-3

Manufactured in the United States of America

Art Producer: Hannah Dickerson
Editor: John Makowski
Production Manager: Holly Haydash

All illustrations used under license from Shutterstock.com

10 9 8 7 6 5 4 3 2 1

This journal belongs to

_____Mandi_____

CONTENTS

Introduction ... viii

How to Use This Journal ... x

SECTION 1 Accept How You Feel ... 1

SECTION 2 Prioritize Your Self-Care ... 21

SECTION 3 Reflect on What Happened ... 41

SECTION 4 Establish Healthy Boundaries ... 63

SECTION 5 Take Small Steps Toward Healing ... 83

A Final Note ... 104

Resources ... 105

References ... 108

INTRODUCTION

The journal you are holding belongs to you and will guide you as you embark on your journey toward healing. Congratulations on taking this step!

When I was approached about creating a journal centered around healing from the trauma of infidelity, I immediately thought, "Well, this is right up my alley," followed by a feeling of interest, intrigue, and trust. It wasn't long ago that I first began creating resources and reflections that supported me around my own healing.

Throughout my years as a licensed marriage and family therapist in private practice in New York City, I have had the pleasure of working with people from diverse backgrounds, cultures, and socioeconomic groups. I have learned over the years that trauma is trauma, and when people come into my office experiencing the effects of the betrayal of infidelity, their feelings, symptoms, and needs are similar. I am humbly reminded of our shared humanity in those moments.

This journal comprises reflections I used during my own healing journey, along with my observations from working for over a decade as a therapist supporting others. This journal can be used alone or in addition to therapy. I use many of the tools in this journal with clients, but it is not meant to be a replacement for therapy. If you are experiencing debilitating or intense emotions, I recommend getting support from a mental health professional. I encourage people to talk to a therapist when going through any major life transition, even if they believe they do not need one.

When I talk about this journal being right up my alley, I am not speaking only as a psychotherapist, but as a fellow human being affected by infidelity. I no longer attach a value of "good" or "bad" to my experiences. Instead, I see my life through the lens of experiences that have led me to a deeper understanding of who I am, what I want, and how I get to show up in the world for myself and others. I did not get there overnight; it was a process of healing my heart by accepting, validating, and transforming my pain.

I often think about a quote from one of my favorite books, *The Alchemist* by Paulo Coelho: "You will never be able to escape your heart, so you better listen to what it has to say." Infidelity creates a heartache and a heartbreak that requires acknowledgment, acceptance, and compassion. Listening to your heart is required for healing to take place.

The fact that you are reading these words speaks to your ability to cultivate resilience and heal. The trauma of infidelity changed you as well as your relationship. You now have an opportunity to ease your pain, heal your heart, and get to know the latest, most authentic version of yourself. You are the creator of your journal and your life. Let's see where your healing journey takes you.

HOW TO USE THIS JOURNAL

First things first: If you have not yet written your name in the "This journal belongs to" section, please do. You get to own how courageous you are being in this part of your healing process. Your interaction with your journal is completely up to you. It has been created with the intention of you working through the sections in order. However, flipping to specific sections or journal elements may support you more at this time. You get to choose.

Your journal has five sections, each including evidence-based practices and therapeutic modalities.

Each section has three practices that are done in your life outside of the journal, most of which are focused on a mind-body approach to healing trauma. These practices are meant to support you in staying grounded and returning to the present moment. There are three exercises that are done inside the journal, focusing on behavioral change, increased understanding, and actionable steps. There are five writing prompts that encourage deep reflection and encourage you to explore answers to questions you may not have thought to ask yourself. Lastly, you will find affirmations throughout the journal. Stating affirmations, especially with visualizations, helps create new neural pathways, changing how you experience life and how you see yourself.

Take your time. There is no rush. Allow yourself to be immersed in your reflection process. I usually recommend completing one or two exercises daily, but you get to choose your process and your pace. Let's begin . . .

I accept all of my feelings and allow them to flow through me.

SECTION 1

ACCEPT HOW YOU FEEL

It is not easy, and it is actually quite courageous, to delve in and take a naked look at your raw emotions, particularly those associated with an experience as painful as infidelity. Congratulations on your decision to begin the process.

It can be hard to name your emotions, especially when you are experiencing so many of them that you might feel numb and have difficulty accessing them. However, on your healing path you can also find the ability to name, understand, validate, and accept all of your emotions with unconditional love, and learn how to process them without judgment, guilt, or shame.

In *Atlas of the Heart*, Brené Brown writes, "The language we use shapes our experiences." She speaks about the importance of understanding and naming our emotions. This first section will support you as you gain more clarity around your feelings.

Let's talk about how that works: In order to accept our feelings, we have to understand them. In order to understand them, we have to name them. In order to name them, we have to admit them. In order to heal, we have to complete that process. Through the use of practices, exercises, affirmations, and prompts all centered on feelings, we will journey through the process of compassionate acceptance together. I am excited for you!

I Accept My Feelings

The following exercise will help you begin to acknowledge and accept how you are feeling. Dr. Paul Ekman described six main types of emotions: enjoyment, sadness, fear, anger, disgust, and contempt. However, there may be other feelings that resonate more for you. Circle any of the feelings in the following list. Then, feel free to add your own feelings to a personalized Acceptance Power Statement for each feeling, which you can begin on this page and continue on a separate piece of paper.

(Sadness)	(Uneasiness)	Disgrace
Lonliness	Happiness	Foolishness
(Hurt)	Excitement	(Regret)
Disappointment	Cheerfulness	Fear
(Loss)	Delight	Insecurity
(Heartbreak)	Bliss	(Nervousness)
(Anger)	Contentment	(Worry)
(Betrayal)	Gratitude	(Shock)
(Rage)	Shame	(Anxiousness)
(Frustration)	Worthlessness	
(Annoyance)	Embarassment	

Acceptance Power Statement

"I accept my feeling of _____. I get to accept this feeling because _____."

You have already taken a major step toward healing and made it to your first prompt. How are you feeling right now, in this moment? What are some thoughts that came up for you around the idea of accepting how you are feeling? Suggestion: Take a couple of deep breaths before you answer.

Pursed Lip Breathing

Excessive thoughts and visualizations about the infidelity can lead to increased anxiety and heart rate. A fast and effective way to lower your heart rate and send a message to your brain to slow down and **accept all the feelings that come up for you** is by practicing breathwork. One popular breathing technique is diaphragmatic or pursed lip breathing. Try three or four mindful breaths.

1. Get comfortable, drop your shoulders, and close your eyes.
2. Take a normal breath in through your nose for a count of two ("inhale, one, two"), allowing your belly to expand.
3. Pucker/purse your lips (whistling motion).
4. Slowly breathe out through your mouth for a count of four ("exhale, one, two, three, four") while pulling your stomach inward.

> Meditation is a helpful tool for maintaining emotional health. Identifying a "happy place" to go to in your mind during meditation creates an opportunity for your mind and body to experience the sensations (joy, peace, etc.) associated with the visualization. Where is your "happy place"? Why did you choose it? How do you feel when you are there?

_____
_____
_____
_____
_____
_____
_____
_____
_____
_____
_____
_____
_____
_____
_____
_____
_____

Understanding My Thoughts and Feelings

Being mindful entails checking in with ourselves when thoughts and feelings arise. The practice of Mindfulness-Based Cognitive Therapy (MBCT) gives us an opportunity to understand why we are

ANTECEDENT (AKA THE TRIGGER)	THOUGHTS	FEELINGS	
Partner doesn't answer their phone.	I hope they are not with someone else/cheating.	Anger, fear, anxiety	

experiencing unpleasant emotions while simultaneously giving ourselves permission to feel and validate them.

Thoughts can come up and then trigger emotions. Sometimes emotions can come first, with thoughts showing up afterward to help us cope with those emotions. Either way, the following chart can help you identify the thoughts/feelings process, while recognizing any judgment or negative self-talk.

SELF-JUDGMENT (AKA NEGATIVE SELF-TALK)	VALIDATING STATEMENT (ACCEPTANT SELF-TALK)
"Why are you afraid? If they are cheating again, you can just leave them!"	*I am feeling anxious and fearful because I have been triggered. It makes sense that I feel this way, since I experienced infidelity in this relationship.*

Accept How You Feel

> I talk to people all the time about the importance of validating the feelings they are experiencing. Have you validated all your feelings? Does negative self-talk take the lead when you acknowledge your feelings? What does the voice in your head sound like? Is it compassionate or a bully?

The Body Scan—Mindfulness Meditation

The mindfulness meditation practice of a body scan is a helpful tool for learning to tune in to your body. The body scan reconnects us to our physical self, allowing us to pick up on sensations we might otherwise ignore.

1. Sit in a comfortable position.
2. Bring awareness to a specific part of your body, starting at your toes.
3. Spend twenty to sixty seconds noticing the sensations in that body part.
4. Take deep breaths, and with each exhale, imagine the tension flowing out of you.
5. When you are ready, move upward to the next part of your body and repeat.
6. After you have scanned your entire body, take a few deep breaths.
7. Slowly open your eyes and thank yourself for prioritizing your well-being in this moment.

Some people experience conflicting emotions after learning about their partner's infidelity. You can shift rapidly from wanting to work things out to feeling extreme anger and wanting to end the relationship. What feelings are you currently experiencing? Do you find yourself judging any of your feelings? If so, which ones and why?

_____
_____
_____
_____
_____
_____
_____
_____
_____
_____
_____
_____
_____
_____
_____
_____

Did You Say "Gratitude"?

Expressing gratitude helps us go from our innate negative mental bias (part of the evolutionary process that helps us detect threats in our environment) to releasing both dopamine and serotonin, the two powerhouse neurotransmitters responsible for happiness. It also helps decrease and regulate oxytocin, the stress hormone associated with sadness and anxiety.

In the aftermath of infidelity, expressing gratitude daily may seem challenging. The great news is that repeatedly sending the positive impulses of gratitude to your brain helps create behavioral and neurocognitive changes.

Let's get started with your gratitude log. Identify five people, places, or things you are grateful for and why. After you are done, make it a habit with a gratitude journal.

I am grateful for _____

because _____.

I am grateful for _____

because _____.

I am grateful for _____

because _____.

I am grateful for _____

because _____.

I am grateful for _____

because _____.

Accepting how you feel is critical to moving through your healing process. What are some of your takeaways, now that you have completed some practices and exercises? Have you noticed a feeling or thought that you were unaware of? Did anything come up during any of the practices? If so, what?

I Am the Observer of My Emotions

This practice of moving from the internalization to the externalization of an emotion, allowing you to take a closer look at it, incorporates narrative therapy and mindfulness. Here is an example.

INTERNALIZATION: *I am anxious.*	EXTERNALIZATION: *I am experiencing anxiety.*

1. Pick an emotion.
2. Find a comfortable position.
3. Close your eyes.
4. Take three deep breaths.
5. Assign a color and form to your emotion.
6. On your next exhale, visualize breathing the emotion out of your body.
7. Imagine seeing your emotion five feet away, in its color and form.
8. Take another deep breath.
9. Ask yourself, "Why is anxiety showing up at this time?"
10. You may take the emotion back later, or it may take another form for you. The goal is to learn how to observe, manage, and accept your emotions.

My feelings are valid and deserve unconditional love and acceptance.

●

My self-care matters, because I matter.

SECTION 2

PRIORITIZE YOUR SELF-CARE

When life feels uncertain, we can pressure ourselves to figure things out in hopes it will make us feel better, ease the pain, and restore our sense of control. An infidelity can leave us hurt and confused. Thankfully, you worked through a lot of your feelings about this in section 1, and your healing will, of course, be an ongoing process.

You need *you* at this time: your time, love, understanding, and care for yourself. While you may have many items on your to-do list, it is vital that you take the time to practice mindfulness exercises and ensure that your emotional needs are met.

This is the type of self-care that involves being mindful, is done with intention, and leaves you feeling lighter, more connected to yourself, and more hopeful. People often ask me what self-care looks like. I describe it as giving yourself permission to engage in activities you enjoy, purely because they are meaningful to you.

In this next section you will create your own definition of self-care and identify activities you authentically enjoy. You will identify barriers to practicing self-care, and gain tools to support you in prioritizing your self-care. You will be reminded that you deserve to be loved and cared for, and who better to show you love than yourself?

Mindful Breath Countdown: Identify Your Needs

This is a short meditation that focuses on identifying your needs within a few minutes. If you want to practice self-care and are not sure where to begin, this mindful practice can support you.

1. Sit or lie down in a comfortable position.
2. Close your eyes and mouth.
3. Take three deep breaths in through your nose and out through your mouth.
4. Take a deep, slow breath in through your nose and mentally say, "Ten."
5. Take a deep, slow breath out through your mouth and mentally say, "Ten."
6. Next inhale nine, exhale nine, and repeat downward until you get to "one, one."
7. Wiggle your fingers and slowly open your eyes.
8. Ask yourself gently, **"What do I need in this moment?"**

When you read that this section focuses on self-care, what are your initial thoughts and feelings? How does the thought of making yourself a priority feel? What do you believe prioritizing yourself will look like?

_____
_____
_____
_____
_____
_____
_____
_____
_____
_____
_____
_____
_____
_____
_____
_____
_____
_____
_____

Name Your Self-Care

Your self-care is a form of self-love that is uniquely your own. The "five love languages," created by Dr. Gary Chapman, are a longtime go-to for helping people identify which expression of love most resonates with them. I have listed them here to get you started with identifying self-care activities tailored to your wants and needs.

RANKING	LOVE LANGUAGE	SELF-CARE DESCRIPTION
1	Words of Affirmation	Developing positive affirmations; creating a "win" journal.
2	Quality Time	Spending time outside; painting for an uninterrupted period.
3	Physical Touch	Taking a warm bath; giving myself a mindful massage; applying lotion.
4	Acts of Service	Making my favorite meal.
5	Receiving Gifts	Buying myself flowers.

Now name yours.

RANKING	LOVE LANGUAGE	SELF-CARE DESCRIPTION
1		
2		
3		
4		
5		

Think about a day that would be a stress-free, carefree delight. A day that is all about you, when you do not have to consider anyone or anything but yourself, with no consequences. What would the name of that day be? What would you do from the moment you woke up until you went to bed?

_____
_____
_____
_____
_____
_____
_____
_____
_____
_____
_____
_____
_____
_____
_____
_____
_____
_____

The Best Gift of All: A Restful Sleep

Sleep is vital to good health and is often negatively impacted by infidelity. Studies show a correlation between depression, poor decision making, and sleep deprivation. According to the National Sleep Foundation (NSF), adults aged eighteen to sixty-four require seven to nine hours of sleep each night. Establishing a sleep ritual can lower stress and stabilize mood.

The following are steps to creating a healthy sleep ritual (one hour before bed):

1. No electronics sixty minutes before bed.
2. Personal hygiene: Take a warm bath (ideally) or wash your face and brush your teeth.
3. Quiet an overactive mind: Make a list of what you want to get done the next day.
4. Meditate for three to five minutes with a visualization to induce pleasant dreams.
5. Drink a warm, non-caffeinated beverage.
6. Write down three things you are grateful for in your gratitude journal.

Many people have opinions regarding self-care; some think it's selfish, while others believe it is a human right. What are some thoughts you have about self-care? Do you have any judgment toward anyone who practices self-care? Is there anyone in your life you admire for the way they care for themselves?

_____

_____

_____

_____

_____

_____

_____

_____

_____

_____

_____

_____

_____

_____

_____

_____

_____

_____

_____

_____

Self-Care Accountability Log

Often when I talk with clients about their self-care, they bring up not having enough time or money for it, or they don't see the importance of it at all. You may already be doing some things for yourself that you are not identifying as self-care. Other times we get so caught up in our day, we skip meals, don't drink enough water, and do not check in with ourselves about how we are feeling. The following chart will help you start a daily habit of self-care. Every day, identify one self-care activity (you can reference the items you identified in the Name Your Self-Care exercise on page 25). Good luck, and enjoy treating yourself with love!

DATE	ACTIVITY
11/1/22	*60-minute mindful time outside.*
11/2/22	*Purchased new resistance bands for my workout.*

Self-care is a form of self-love that looks different for each person. One of the first steps in identifying your personal forms of self-care is to remind yourself of what you enjoy doing. What are you doing when you feel most relaxed? When do you feel most yourself? What does loving yourself in all your authenticity look like?

Create Morning Rituals

Rituals help align our values and priorities with our actions. Prioritizing your self-care sounds great in theory, and in this section, we are focusing on creating morning habits and routines that turn that theory into action. Rituals cue us on what we can expect by providing structure. At a time when there is increased uncertainty in your life, rituals can keep you feeling grounded and safe.

Observe your mornings for one week. Pay attention to the time you wake up and the first things you do. Is there anything you can do to make your morning go more smoothly?

The following week, add meditation, breathwork, or a yoga practice of at least fifteen minutes every morning. Adjust as needed, keeping at least one mindful activity daily.

The trauma of infidelity can lead one to become hyperfocused on both the other person and trying to figure out what to do next. Although it may be challenging, this is a crucial time to be an active participant in your healing process through self-care. Do you anticipate any barriers to practicing self-care? What might get in the way?

_____
_____
_____
_____
_____
_____
_____
_____
_____
_____
_____
_____
_____
_____
_____
_____
_____
_____
_____
_____

Morning Commitments

Using some of the ideas from your observations in the Create Morning Rituals practice on page 34, take fifteen minutes to sit and think about what your ideal morning would look like, and then write down three rituals you would like to commit to every morning. There is a lot of research on the value of making your bed as soon as you wake up in the morning, and how it signals to your brain that you have already accomplished the first task of the day. Are there any other rituals you would like to identify and commit to? As few as three ten-minute daily rituals can set the tone for the entire day. Start off with three and see how it feels.

I commit to the morning ritual of _____ .

I commit to the morning ritual of _____ .

I commit to the morning ritual of _____ .

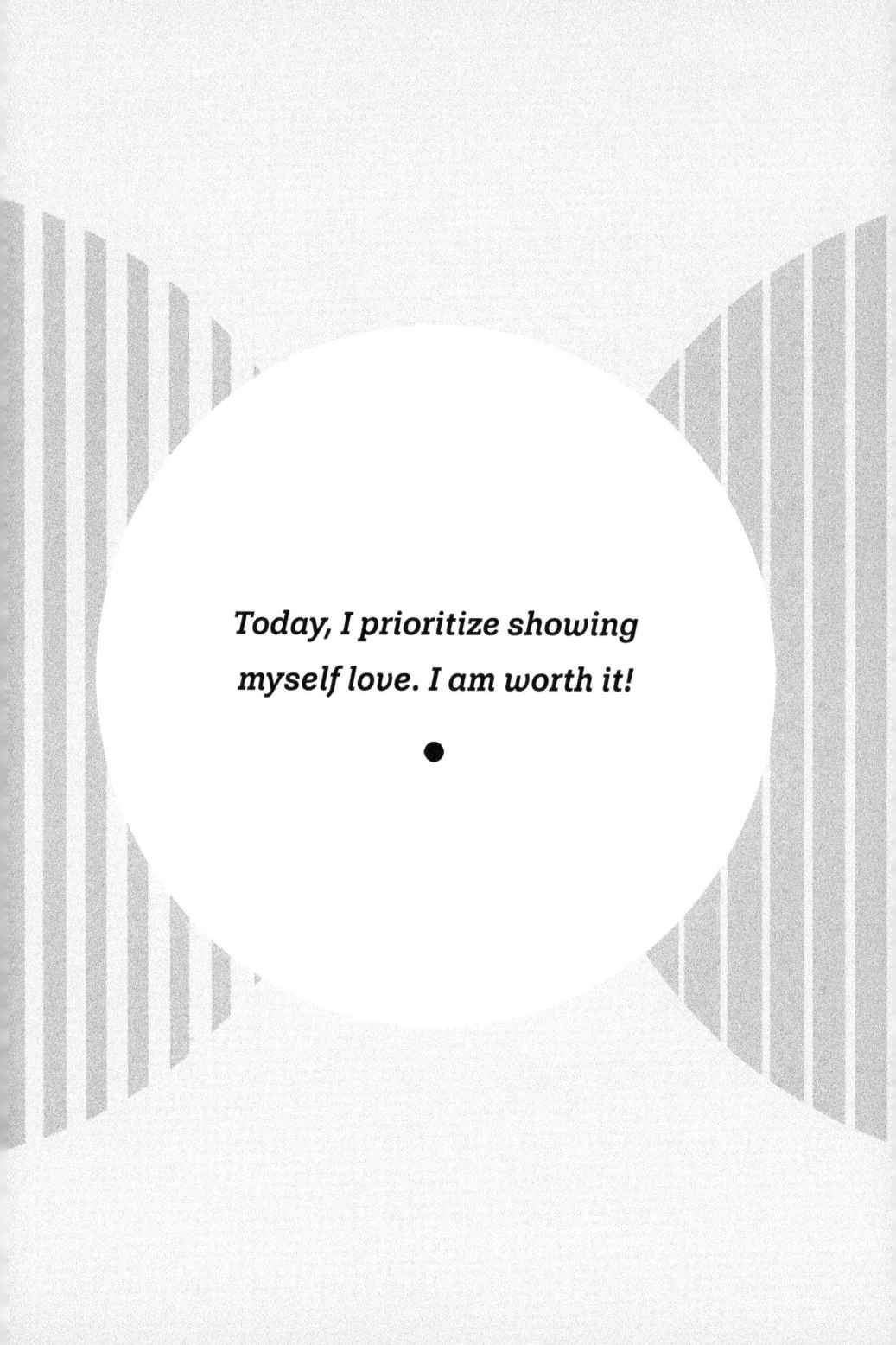

Today, I prioritize showing myself love. I am worth it!

I love wholeheartedly and deserve reciprocity.

SECTION 3

REFLECT ON WHAT HAPPENED

Reflection helps us gain insight to support our moving forward in life. Welcome to the section on introspection, reflection, shoe swapping, and accountability without judgment, as you explore how infidelity touched your relationship and where you are in the reflection process now.

A relationship is co-created by two people who are always feeding the interpersonal dynamic. In this section you will put yourself in your partner's shoes for the purpose of understanding why they went outside your relationship. While there is no justifying or excusing a breach of trust like this, understanding the drivers of their behavior can provide you with a deeper understanding of yourself, as well as the dynamics in your relationship.

When one partner commits infidelity, both partners have usually been experiencing unmet needs. While this is not always the case, understanding both of your love languages and your attachment styles may create an opportunity for you to heal.

Infidelity does not have to mean the end of your relationship, although sometimes it is. Whether you choose to work through the infidelity and stay together or you decide that the betrayal means the end of the relationship, what you learn from this experience will be valuable for how you navigate your life. Let's begin.

What's Your Attachment Style?

In the 1950s, psychiatrist and psychoanalyst John Bowlby founded attachment theory, which highlights how the attachment we experienced with our primary caregivers influences our relationships as adults. Understanding your attachment style can provide additional insight into your relationship. Circle the statements here that resonate with you most:

1. I easily trust others.
2. I exhibit confusing and unpredictable behavior.
3. I fear being alone.
4. I avoid emotional intimacy.
5. I know how to regulate my emotions.
6. I have a tendency to cling to others.
7. I have a hard time sharing my feelings.
8. I fear rejection.
9. I am comfortable being alone.
10. I need validation from others.
11. I can be dismissive of others.

Answers 1, 5, and 9: Secure people are emotionally stable and expressive, thrive in a relationship and are also comfortable being on their own, have a positive view of themselves and others, and cultivate healthy and honest relationships.

Answers 2 and 8: Disorganized (also known as fearful avoidant) people want emotional closeness and intimacy while simultaneously fearing it, send mixed signals, and display unstable behaviors in relationships.

Answers 3, 6, and 10: Anxious (also known as preoccupied) people seek responsiveness and approval from their partner, are preoccupied with the relationship, are insecure, and can be clingy.

Answers 4, 7, and 11: Avoidant (also known as dismissive) people can have high self-esteem, do not want others to depend on them, are independent, have a lone wolf mentality, avoid emotional closeness, and hide emotions.

There are four attachment styles: secure (generally trusting and positive), avoidant (strong sense of independence and dismissive of others), anxious (have difficulty being alone and are seeking validation), and disorganized (confusing and contradictory, going from clingy to independent behavior). What type of attachment style do you have? How did your attachment style form? How does it play out in your relationship?

Getting Back to the Present

Deliberately recalling the events of the infidelity you experienced may bring up uncomfortable emotions. If you experience intense emotions at any point during your reflection, take a breath and observe your emotions and thoughts. This quick mindfulness exercise will bring you back to the present moment.

1. Observe the stressful thought or emotion.
2. Identify the physical sensations related to the thought or emotion.
3. Take a deep breath while focusing on the areas of your body that are experiencing the sensations.
4. Meet the sensations with openness, as an opportunity for increased self-awareness.
5. Inhale. Visualize bringing comfort to that area of your body.
6. Exhale. Visualize your body releasing the stressful energy.
7. Take another deep breath, roll your shoulders, and open your eyes.

In the Name Your Self-Care exercise on page 25, you identified your love languages to support your self-care. Love languages also play an important role in how you and your partner experience each other. What is your partner's love language? Were you and your partner showing each other love in your individual love languages prior to the infidelity? If so, how?

It's a Process: Separating the Facts from Thoughts and Emotions

Your reflection on the infidelity may be blurred by thoughts and strong emotions. This exercise will help you externalize the events by identifying them as objective facts to support you with understanding your thoughts and accompanying emotions.

Column one: Write down the facts.
Column two: Write down the accompanying thoughts.
Column three: Identify the emotions that accompanied the thought.

	FACTS/ WHAT HAPPENED	THOUGHTS	EMOTIONS
1	They had been working later at the office.	They were trying to make more money for our future.	Lucky, worthy of being loved, and appreciated.
2	They were spending nights with someone else and not at work.	They have been lying to me for months. How could I be so stupid?	Betrayed, hurt, foolish, and angry.

CONTINUED >

Reflect on What Happened

CONTINUED >

FACTS/ WHAT HAPPENED	THOUGHTS	EMOTIONS
1		
2		
3		
4		

After discovering an infidelity, we tend to focus on what went wrong, but acknowledging your relationship strengths can support you when deciding how to move forward. What aspects of your relationship do you appreciate? What would you consider some of your couple strengths?

Letting Go of My Story to Understand Yours

The following visualization gives you an opportunity to put yourself in your partner's shoes by releasing your perspective and enabling yourself to see theirs. Your goal is to gain a deeper understanding of why they went outside the relationship, while continuing to honor your own experience and emotions.

1. Find a comfortable position. Close your eyes.
2. Imagine you and your partner sitting across from each other, writing letters to share your individual perspectives about what led to the infidelity.
3. Visualize giving each other compassionate eye contact, then exchanging letters.
4. Envision yourself reading their letter with an open heart and compassion.
5. As you read, allow yourself to experience feelings of calm and acceptance.
6. Take a deep breath, feel the calm within your body, and visualize yourself handing the letter back.
7. Open your eyes.

During your visualization practice on page 53, you were able to calmly exchange vulnerable letters and share your individual perspectives about the infidelity. Based on what your partner has previously shared regarding the reasons why they did what they did, as well as your observations, what do you believe your partner's perspective is? What do you imagine their letter would say?

What I've Learned along the Way

In every hardship, there is a lesson. If we practice reflection, we learn from our experiences. Infidelity is an experience that, although traumatic, is rich with lessons regarding who we are and what we want in our relationships. Complete the following to help identify what you have learned from this experience.

When **[this happened]**, I **[felt/did this]**, and I learned **[this about myself or relationships]**.

When *I found out my partner cheated*, I *felt like I lost my identity*, and I learned *that I was relying on someone else to determine my worth.*

When *my partner moved out*, I *was dependent on myself*, and I learned *that I am resilient.*

When _____,

I _____,

and I learned _____.

When _____,

I _____,

and I learned _____.

When _____,

I _____,

and I learned _____.

According to psychotherapist Esther Perel, "People cheat on each other in a hundred different ways: indifference, emotional neglect, contempt, lack of respect, years of refusal of intimacy. Cheating doesn't begin to describe the ways that people let each other down." Other than the infidelity, in what ways has your partner let you down? How have you let your partner down?

Reflect on What Happened

Saying Custom Affirmations Based on Your Lessons

The lessons learned from the experience of infidelity are valuable. Affirmations created directly from what you have learned will support you in developing new neural pathways, which leads to a change in perspective. Identify two lessons you wrote in the What I've Learned along the Way exercise on page 56 and create a custom affirmation.

Example:
Lesson learned: "I was relying on someone else to determine my worth."
Affirmation: *I determine my worth and I am worthy of love.*
Lesson learned: "I learned that I am resilient."
Affirmation: *I am resilient.*

The key to affirmations is repetition. Practice saying the affirmations at least twice daily and allow yourself to feel the positive emotions they evoke.

Your lesson: _____
_____.

Your affirmation: _____
_____.

Your lesson: _____
_____.

Your affirmation: _____
_____.

*I am worthy of love and
deserving of truth.*

●

I honor myself through the implementation of my boundaries.

SECTION 4

ESTABLISH HEALTHY BOUNDARIES

Infidelity is a breach of trust, an ultimate crossed boundary, and a shock to your emotional and family systems. Creating healthy boundaries that make you feel like you are protecting, honoring, and keeping yourself safe is imperative to your healing process. As you move forward and create a secure and strong sense of self, creating boundaries will ensure that your personal, emotional, and physical well-being are intact.

In this section you will address your relationship with setting boundaries, learn how to create them, identify when they are needed, and practice implementing them. You get to decide what you are comfortable sharing, how you would like to move forward, and what you need to make that happen. The people around you will have their opinions, and your openness to accepting their guidance/advice is completely up to you. Some will tell you it is more courageous to stay, while others will tell you that it is more courageous to end the relationship. You, and no one else, get to decide what your courage looks like. Let's begin identifying your healthy boundaries.

Visualizing Your Safe Bubble

Boundaries make us feel safe. Establishing boundaries protects us from being taken advantage of and ensures that we are honoring ourselves and our needs. If you find yourself absorbing the negativity of others, feeling overwhelmed by their expectations, and having a challenging time protecting your energy, visualizing yourself in a safe bubble of light may help.

1. Get in a comfortable position and close your eyes.
2. Envision yourself surrounded by a bright bubble of light.
3. In this bubble you are safe; no one can penetrate it.
4. Identify the person you want to protect your energy from.
5. Visualize the other person as separate from you, in their own bubble of light.
6. Send loving energy to yourself and the other person.
7. Remind yourself that you are safe.
8. Slowly open your eyes.

The thought of setting boundaries can seem daunting and create feelings of anxiety, especially if this was not modeled for you as a child. What did boundaries look like in your household when you were growing up? Do you remember your caregivers establishing boundaries? If so, what were they?

_____
_____
_____
_____
_____
_____
_____
_____
_____
_____
_____
_____
_____
_____
_____
_____
_____

Boundary or No Boundary: How Will I Know?

The following table will support you in identifying when a boundary may be useful. Any time you experience a strong emotion like overwhelm, resentment, anger, or despair, take some time to write

I FEEL...	WHEN?	WHO?	
Anxious and disrespected.	*I receive nonstop calls because they want to talk.*	*My spouse.*	

it in the chart provided. Then walk your way across the row to determine whether you would benefit from creating a boundary in this situation.

WHAT DO I WANT?	THE BOUNDARY I SET AND ITS CONSEQUENCE
No calls or texts from them unless initiated by me.	*I feel pressured and get anxious when you contact me repeatedly. If you continue to reach out, I will no longer consider reconciliation because I am experiencing your behavior as disrespectful.*

Research shows that establishing healthy boundaries after the trauma of an infidelity supports maintaining your emotional and mental health. It is a form of self-love and sets clear expectations for everyone involved. How does the idea of setting boundaries with others make you feel? How do you think you will feel once people begin honoring your boundaries?

Empty Chair

In the Boundary or No Boundary exercise on page 66, you identified boundaries you wanted to establish and created scripts. These scripts will enable you to practice sharing your boundaries clearly and effectively. The empty chair technique that originated in Gestalt therapy (therapy focused on the present rather than the past) is used often because it allows a person to practice expressing their thoughts and feelings to another person without that person needing to be in the room. Give it a try.

1. Read over your prepared script.
2. Prepare two chairs, one for yourself and an empty chair for the person you will be "talking" to.
3. Direct your words and gestures toward the chair, as if the person were seated in it.
4. Accept without judgment any intense emotions that may arise.
5. Continue this exercise until you feel ready for the actual conversation.

Turning to your loved ones after learning about the infidelity can support you and your healing process. People often feel shame regarding the infidelity, even when their partner had the affair. What is your comfort level with reaching out to people in your circle of family and friends? Is shame or any other negative emotion preventing you from seeking support?

What's My Comfort Level?

The following checklist can help you identify what you feel comfortable sharing with others. Family and friends can offer

QUESTIONS	SHARE? YES/NO	WITH WHOM?	
How long has the affair been happening?			
Do you know the person they had the affair with?			
Where did your partner meet the person?			
Did you notice changes in your partner's behavior?			
Is your partner leaving you for this person?			
Did your partner end the affair?			
Do you plan to work things out or separate?			
Have you been tested for STIs?			
Where is the person they cheated with from?			
Are you planning on going to couples therapy?			
Have you checked your partner's bank statements?			

unsolicited advice and ask questions you may find intrusive, however well-intended they may be. Fill out the following chart.

	HOW MUCH?

In the Empty Chair practice on page 70, you practiced your script and got more comfortable with having conversations regarding your boundaries. Whom did you envision in the chair? How did you feel stating your boundary out loud? Did you stick to the script? Did any of your emotions surprise you?

The Self-Hug: The Hug That's Always Available

Hugs evoke feelings of safety and security. They also make us feel better by releasing endorphins and increasing our production of dopamine. It can get tricky when the person we usually turn to for hugs is the person who made us feel unsafe. Thankfully, you can get the same benefits from a self-hug. It may not come naturally at first, but don't judge it. Give it a try!

1. Identify what kind of hug you want. Soft? Soothing? Firm?
2. In a natural and comfortable way, fold your arms across your body.
3. Rest your hands on your upper arms or shoulders, or rub them up and down.
4. Add comforting words if you desire, such as, "Everything is going to be okay."
5. Continue for as long as it feels good.

In the What's My Comfort Level? exercise on page 72, you completed a checklist of what questions you feel comfortable answering, how much you are open to sharing, and whom you are comfortable sharing with. Were any of the questions listed on the checklist triggering? If so, which questions made you feel uncomfortable? Why?

Creating Boundary Scripts

Scripts are not just for actors; they help us prepare to have calm conversations that may otherwise be emotionally charged.

In the Boundary or No Boundary exercise on page 66, you created the boundaries. Here are the steps to create the script:

1. Offer acknowledgment.
2. State your needs ("I" statements).
3. Describe clear boundaries.
4. Establish a consequence.

Example:

1. *I recognize your desire for closeness.*
2. *I need to feel safe to sleep in the bed with you.*
3. *I ask that you sleep in the other room until I let you know otherwise.*
4. *If you come in the bed or continue to ask me about it, I am going to ask you to find another place to stay.*

Your Script:

1. Acknowledgment: _____.

2. Need: _____.

3. Boundary: _____.

4. Consequence: _____.

Establish Healthy Boundaries

My boundaries are a reflection of self-love.

The healing energy of love flows through me effortlessly.

SECTION 5

TAKE SMALL STEPS TOWARD HEALING

You are not the same person today that you were before the infidelity. This experience was a catalyst for change and a transformational experience for you and for your relationship. Accepting that truth will allow you to embrace the new, more self-actualized version of yourself with compassion, curiosity, and unconditional self-love.

Learning to trust again will be both challenging and rewarding. You deserve to experience the feeling of safety that self-trust provides. People often seek closure or the ability to forgive in the hope of moving forward without bitterness. My experience has taught me that what most people are truly seeking is to heal their heart, and to keep it open. There is no room for bitterness in a healed heart.

This section is designed to support you when growing your self-trust, healing your heart from the infidelity, and identifying what you want and need to move forward, with or without your partner. You will be given an opportunity to get to know the new authentic version of yourself and create next steps in your healing process that are aligned with the life you want to live.

Hello, Creator. Create.

A Healed Heart

Identify all your feelings and write them in the PRESENT Heart. These emotions can be a mixed bag of rage, fear, love, and more. Let it all out and include everything you are currently feeling. If you are struggling with identifying how you feel, leave the space empty for now.

PRESENT Heart

Rewrite the words that bring you joy from the PRESENT Heart into the HEALED Heart and include new words that represent how you want to feel. Include activities and people that evoke feelings of happiness and gratitude, even if you are not currently feeling this way. Lastly, take any words that make you feel a negative emotion and write them outside the heart. The HEALED Heart should represent all that you want to keep in your heart.

HEALED Heart

In therapy, I often hear clients share that they want closure. People usually have an idea of what closure is "supposed" to look like and how it "should" feel. Do you believe you need closure to move forward? If so, what does closure look like for you? What do you believe closure will help you achieve?

Healed Heart Visualization

According to author and researcher Joe Dispenza, "You can't wait for that healing to feel wholeness. You have to feel wholeness for that healing to occur." Using your full HEALED Heart from the exercise on page 84, repeat the following practice daily to make your conscious intentions subconscious and create new neural pathways.

1. Visualize yourself lying in the grass with the sun shining brightly.
2. Envision the beautiful HEALED Heart, filled with all the joy you identified, exuding from the sun and entering your heart space.
3. Feel the warmth in your body.
4. Experience the bliss of a full heart.
5. Think about how it feels to be so complete.
6. Stay there as long as it feels comfortable, then open your eyes.

In his book *The Mastery of Love*, Don Miguel Ruiz states, "Forgiveness is for your own mental healing. You will forgive because you feel compassion for yourself. Forgiveness is an act of self-love." Do you believe you need to forgive your partner for your heart to heal? Why or why not? Is there anything you need to forgive yourself for?

4-7-8 Breathing Technique

Knowing you can keep yourself safe creates self-trust. Having tools to self-soothe, immediately slow down your heart rate, and keep anxiety at bay in times of high stress is empowering. An immediate feeling of deep relaxation while energizing your cells by increasing your oxygen intake and expelling carbon dioxide from your lungs can be achieved by using a yogic technique known as 4-7-8 breathing, developed by Dr. Andrew Weil.

1. Get comfortable.
2. Place your tongue on the roof of your mouth, right behind your teeth.
3. Keep your mouth closed and breathe in through your nose (count of four).
4. Hold your breath (count of seven).
5. Let your lips part, and exhale through your mouth while making a whooshing sound (count of eight).
6. Repeat four more times.

I Trust Myself

Trust is necessary for safety. Although trust may be challenging to access at this time, you will learn to trust others again. This process truly begins with trusting yourself. In this exercise, please list concerns you have that cause anxiety, then counter them with a statement of self-trust. This exercise reinforces the message that when concerns come up in your body and mind, you know how to keep yourself safe. Using the 4-7-8 Breathing Technique (page 91) can prepare you for this exercise.

Example:
I am concerned that *I will not be able to heal*.
I trust that *if I continue to struggle, I will seek help from a mental health professional*.

I am concerned that _____.

I trust that _____.

I am concerned that _____.

I trust that _____.

I am concerned that _____.

I trust that _____.

I am concerned that _____.

I trust that _____.

As a therapist, I understand the importance of seeking support when experiencing a major life transition/disruption. Infidelity can lead to Post-Infidelity Stress Disorder (PISD), with symptoms including trust issues, sleep disturbance, and changes in personality. Who is currently supporting you? Do you believe you would benefit from therapy? What would your therapeutic goals be?

A Message from Your Future Self Visualization

This mindfulness meditation will support you in envisioning your future, as you come face to face with the healed version of yourself. Future you will have a useful message to share regarding the steps they took to heal.

1. Sit comfortably, eyes closed, and breathe deeply.
2. Imagine yourself walking into a room filled with people gathered for a joyous occasion.
3. You see future you smiling and engaging with people.
4. Observe how future you looks, moves, laughs, etc.
5. Future you makes eye contact with you, smiles, and walks over.
6. They gently take your hand, embrace you, and whisper words of wisdom in your ear.
7. They slowly walk back to the other guests, and you walk out of the room.
8. Take a deep breath and open your eyes.

Things Observed about My Future Self

Envisioning your future healed self will support you in moving courageously in the present, as you remain steadfast and consistent in your self-care and introspection. This acceptance of the present and hope for the future will support you in building a new narrative/plan about who you are and the life you are creating.

Let's explore what came up for you during A Message from Your Future Self Visualization practice on page 95.

1. How did present me feel during the practice?

   _____

2. What did I observe about future me? How did they appear? Smell? Move?

   _____

3. How did I feel when we made eye contact?

   _____

4. What sensations did I feel when we embraced?

   _____

5. What words of wisdom did future me offer to help me heal?

   _____

6. Who did future me become?

   _____

According to psychotherapist Esther Perel, "Once the infidelity happens, it is the end of that marriage." You can either create a new relationship together, or decide to part ways. There is no going back to the old version of your relationship. At this point, are you thinking about repairing or ending the relationship? Would you consider couples therapy? Why or why not?

According to bell hooks, "No matter what has happened in our past, when we open our hearts to love we can live as if born again, not forgetting the past but seeing it in a new way." How open was your heart to giving and receiving love before the infidelity? What would it take for you to open your heart again?

_____

_____

_____

_____

_____

_____

_____

_____

_____

_____

_____

_____

_____

_____

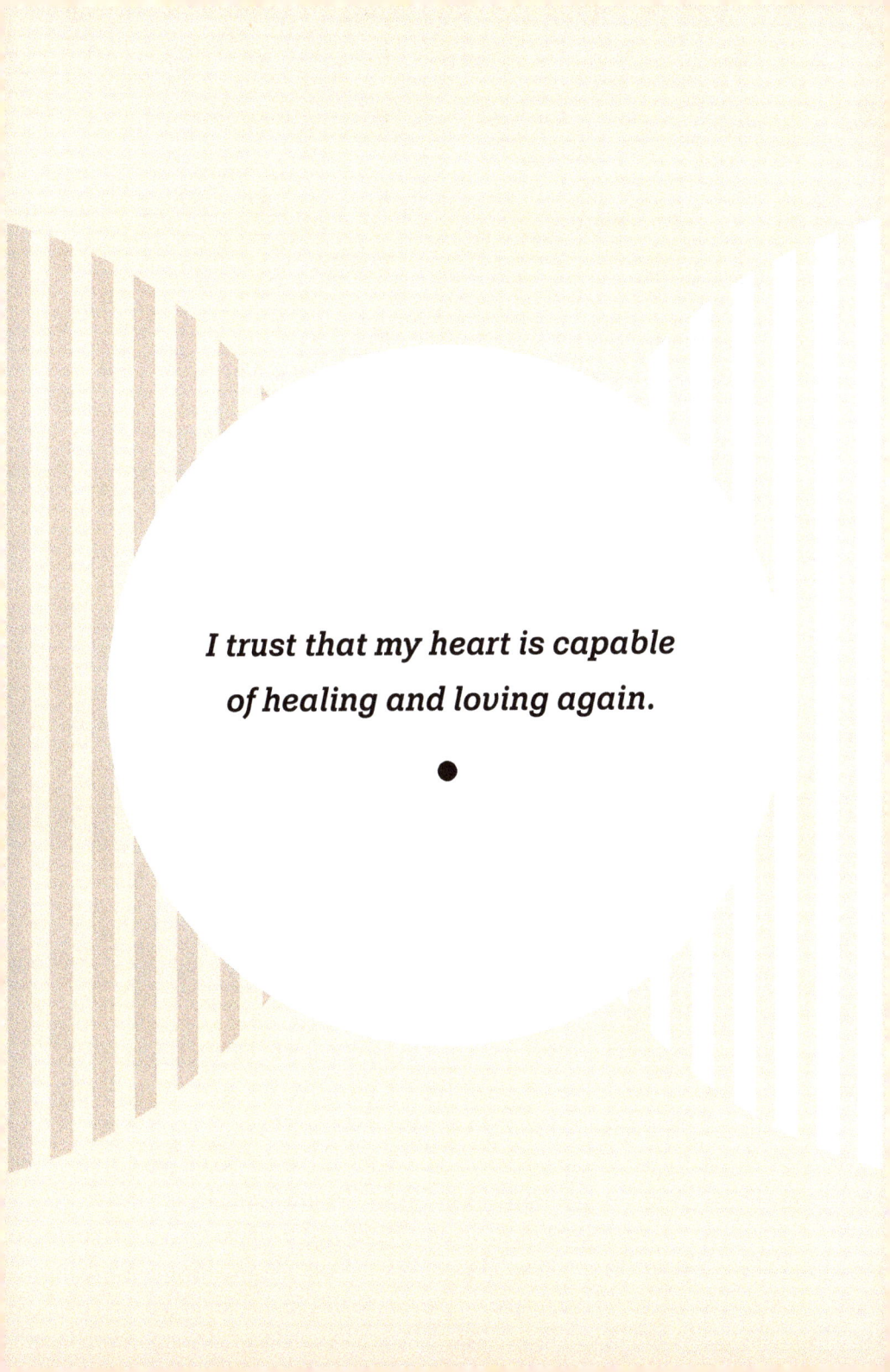

I trust that my heart is capable of healing and loving again.

●

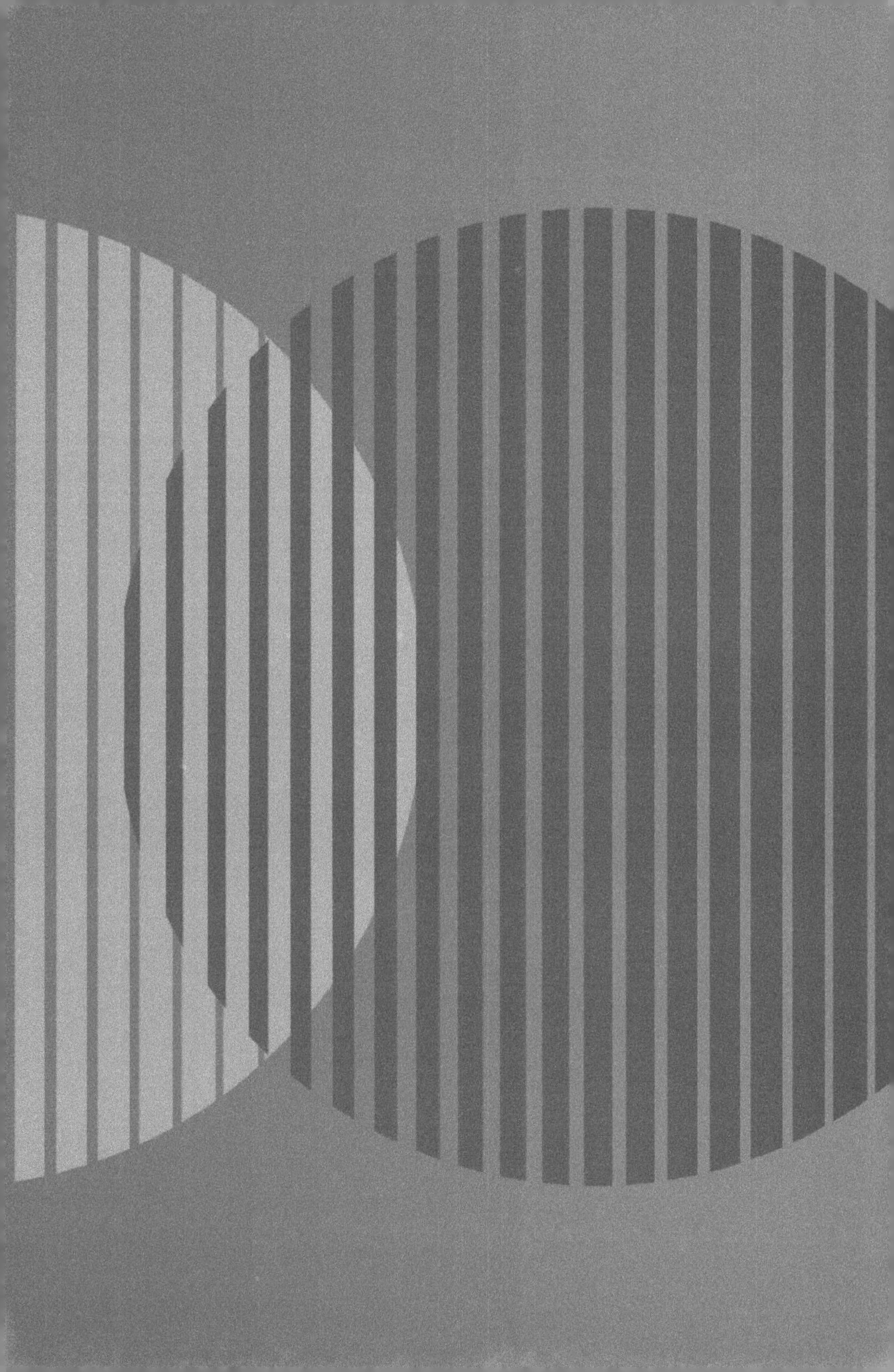

A FINAL NOTE

Deep inhale. Slow exhale. Smile. Congratulations on showing up for yourself and completing your journal! Whether you decide to stay with your partner and heal your relationship or you choose to part ways, you have acquired tools that will support you with moving forward.

Your journal is now a personalized resource. Think of it as your tool kit. The exercises and practices will remain relevant. There may have been sections that brought up uncomfortable emotions, and by validating them, you grew in acceptance and self-love. Some techniques may have resonated more than others. Continue to use them to deepen your mind-body awareness and to help you self-soothe during challenging times.

The duality of life is inherent to our human experience. Inevitably, we will experience moments of joy and moments of pain. There is no one "right" path for every couple or every person.

Where do you go from here? You get to decide. You may use your journal as a resource, begin a new healing modality, or reach out to a therapist or close friend for support. The possibilities are endless. You have been incredibly courageous thus far. May your self-love be limitless. Let's see where your journey continues to take you!

RESOURCES

Apps

Bearable.app (Mood, sleep, and exercise tracker)

Gottman Card Decks (Relationship app)

Headspace.com (Meditation)

Insighttimer.com (Free live yoga and meditation)

Love Nudge (Five love languages relationship app)

Books

Atlas of the Heart: Mapping Meaningful Connection and the Language of Human Experience by Brené Brown

Attached: The New Science of Adult Attachment and How It Can Help You Find—And Keep—Love by Amir Levine, MD, and Rachel S. F. Heller, MA

Daring Greatly: How the Courage to Be Vulnerable Transforms the Way We Live, Love, Parent, and Lead by Brené Brown

Getting the Love You Want: A Guide for Couples by Harville Hendrix, PhD, and Helen LaKelly Hunt, PhD

Books *(continued)*

Mating in Captivity: Reconciling the Erotic & the Domestic by Esther Perel

The 5 Love Languages: The Secret to Love that Lasts by Gary Chapman, PhD

The Four Agreements: A Practical Guide to Personal Freedom by Don Miguel Ruiz

The State of Affairs: Rethinking Infidelity by Esther Perel

Podcasts for Couples

Small Things Often with Julie and John Gottman (gottman.com/podcast)

Unlocking Us with Brené Brown (brenebrown.com/podcast-show/unlocking-us)

Where Should We Begin? with Esther Perel (estherperel.com/podcast)

Podcasts for Self-Love

Room to Grow with Emily Gough (podcasts.apple.com/us/podcast/room-to-grow-podcast-with-emily-gough/id1402942080)

The Road to Self-Love with Paul Fishman (roadtoselflove.libsyn.com)

The Self Love Fix Podcast with Beatrice Kamau (beatricekamau.com/podcast)

Websites

BreneBrown.com (Self-help/relationships)

Christina-Lopes.com (Self-love/heart alchemy)

EstherPerel.com (Couples/relationships)

5LoveLanguages.com (Quiz on love languages)

Gottman.com (Couples/relationships)

YourPersonality.net/attachment (Comprehensive 128-question quiz on attachment)

Mental Health Resources/Support

Psychology Today (Therapist directory)

Suicide and Crisis Lifeline (Call 988 for 24 hour support)

REFERENCES

Annesley, Mike. *Happiness the Mindful Way: A Practical Guide*. London: DK, 2015.

Brown, Brené. *Atlas of the Heart: Mapping Meaningful Connection and the Language of Human Experience*. New York: Penguin Random House LLC, 2021.

Coelho, Paulo. *The Alchemist*. New York: HarperCollins, 1993.

Croxton, Sean. "Dr. Joe Dispenza: 'The Moment You Start Feeling Wholeness, Your Healing Begins.'" *The Quote of the Day Show*. June 15, 2020. seancroxton.com/quote-of-the-day/900.

Dean, Mary Elizabeth. "What Is Post Infidelity Stress Disorder?" BetterHelp. Last modified April 6, 2022. betterhelp.com/advice/stress/what-is-post-infidelity-stress-disorder.

Ekman, Paul. *Emotions Revealed: Recognizing Faces and Feelings to Improve Communication and Emotional Life*. New York: Times Books, 2003.

Fletcher, Jenna. "How to Use 4-7-8 Breathing for Anxiety." *Medical News Today*. February 12, 2019. medicalnewstoday.com/articles/324417.

Gottman, John M. *The Science of Trust: Emotional Attunement for Couples*. New York: Norton, 2011.

Hendrix, Harville, and Helen LaKelly Hunt. *Getting the Love You Want: A Guide for Couples*. New York: Henry Holt and Company LLC, 2019.

hooks, bell. *All About Love: New Visions*. New York: William Morrow and Company, Inc., 2001.

Kim, John. "How to Get Closure." *Psychology Today*. March 17, 2020. psychologytoday.com/us/blog/the-angry-therapist/202003/how-get-closure.

Krouse, Lauren. "The Link Between Sleep and Depression." *Verywell Health*. February 7, 2021. verywellhealth.com/the-link-between-sleep-and-depression-5093051.

Louie, Sam. "5 Ways to Recover From Infidelity." *Psychology Today*. October 3, 2019. psychologytoday.com/us/blog/minority-report/201910/5-ways-recover-infidelity.

Miguel Ruiz, Don, and Janet Mills. *The Mastery of Love: A Practical Guide to the Art of Relationship*. San Rafael, CA: Amber-Allen Publishing, 1999.

National Sleep Foundation. "How Much Sleep Do You Really Need?" October 1, 2020. thensf.org/how-many-hours-of-sleep-do-you-really-need.

Neff, Kristin. *Self-Compassion: The Proven Power of Being Kind to Yourself*. New York: William Morrow, 2011.

Perel, Esther. *The State of Affairs: Rethinking Infidelity*. New York: HarperCollins Publishers, 2017.

Raypole, Crystal. "How to Do a Body Scan Meditation (and Why You Should)." *Healthline*. March 26, 2020. healthline.com/health/body-scan-meditation.

Rothschild, Babette. *8 Keys to Safe Trauma Recovery: Take-Charge Strategies to Empower Your Healing.* New York: Norton, 2010.

Soni, Akanksha. "Gestalt Therapy: Why & How 'Empty Chair Technique' Is Used?" CalmSage. August 21, 2020. calmsage.com/gestalt-therapy-why-how-empty-chair-technique-is-used.

Temple, Della. *Tame Your Inner Critic: Find Peace and Contentment to Live Your Life on Purpose.* Woodbury, MN: Llewellyn, 2019.

Acknowledgments

My heart is thankful to my parents, Joe and Gladys, for their love and commitment to our family. My brother Joe's encouragement. Mariah's compassionate heart. Niko's ambitious spirit. The two Luz's that illuminate my soul. My TF for joining me in the canoe. They all inspire me to be a better human. Lastly, I have gratitude for all my life experiences, including the heartbreaks, because they have taught me what life is all about: love.

About the Author

Tamara Thompson is a licensed marriage and family therapist in private practice in New York City, where she sees clients, holds workshops, paints, and writes a popular blog. She graduated with honors from Iona College and is a Clinical Fellow of the AAMFT. Since 2008, Tamara has supported individuals with healing, self-actualization, and living their purpose. She specializes in helping couples navigate life transitions that inevitably impact relationships. Tamara is passionate about living authentically and creating authentic relationships.

CPSIA information can be obtained
at www.ICGtesting.com
Printed in the USA
JSHW041728250723
45358JS00010B/392

9 781685 392963